T0072411

Write a Letter
To God?

Linda Kay Mullinax

WestBow
PRESS
A DIVISION OF THOMAS NELSON

WestBow Press books may be ordered through booksellers or by contacting:

WestBow Press
A Division of Thomas Nelson
1663 Liberty Drive
Bloomington, IN 47403
www.westbowpress.com
1-(866) 928-1240

ISBN: 978-1-4497-4479-3 (sc)
Library of Congress Control Number: 2012905537

Printed in the United States of America

WestBow Press rev. date: 4/02/2012

This book is dedicated to GOD for encouraging me and being here for me each day. He inspired me to write this book to help others.

To my husband, Thomas, who is the love of my life and for all the notes he leaves me each morning. I love you.

How in the world would you write a letter to God, you might ask? Well, you can't mail it to him, not that I know of. I really don't know of any way to get a letter to God. There is one way, but you would have to die and take it to him yourself.

In the Bible it says the way to do that is to confess our sins and ask Jesus to come into our hearts then we would be able to see him personally. If we die in our sins, that letter will burn up in the hot flames of Hell. I seriously do not recommend going that route because God will not be there.

You cannot mail your letter to God by way of the mail carrier. He or she would probably think you are one brick shy of a load. Nor can you expect to take it to the post office and find an outgoing box that says *Letter to God*. Take my word for it that outgoing box will not be there. I was in New York, the first of December, with our church friends until Thursday night and there wasn't a box like that there before I left to go on our trip. I'm sure that kind of news would've made the front page of the newspaper.

I must tell you a little about my New York trip. Before I do I want to tell you a little about myself. My name is Linda Mulllinax and I live in Gastonia, North Carolina which is about twenty miles from Charlotte. I have fibromyalgia. I have had this invisible disease for 28 years. Oh, yes, I wrote a book about it too. The name of the book is It's Okay To Hurt-My Life With Fibromyalgia. If you have this terrible disease I hope you will get a copy.

I have one sister, Penny, and she is a mother and grandmother. She is older than me by two years. She hates it when I tell that. So guess what? I put it in this book too. Hey, she is my sister what can she do? I love her with all my heart and I am guilty of not telling her that more than I do.

I would like to congratulate Penny on her retirement on Friday March 9th. She has worked long and hard for this day.

Friends, take time out of your busy schedule to tell your family you love them. Give them a phone call or just a card will do. They may not be here tomorrow and neither may you.

I am a Christian and the Lord saved my soul in 1975 several months before our precious daughter, Cindy, died. She had acute lymphatic leukemia.

If you have had a loved one die from cancer or some other serious problem, I have walked in your shoes. I know the pain you are suffering. It is never easy to lose a loved one whether they are young or old. The pain isn't any less. In our minds we always believe that we will pass away before our children.

Right when you think you have your pain and loneliness under control, you remember something your loved one said or did and the pain starts all over again.

I put my faith and trust in God to carry me through each day. His strength and power is greater than mine or yours. God knows your heart broke the day you lost that precious loved one. He has gone through the same thing. I'll tell you more about it later on in the book.

Please, don't give up. I know you want to because I did. At times the pain just seems too much for you to handle. That is where our faith comes in.

I will be telling you about going to Webster for checking what the meaning of some words are. My Webster's Dictionary is published in 1980 so you can see I probably need to get an up dated one. But I am quite certain that the meanings are still the same. Books may change in size and shape but the meanings of the words still stay the same.

Webster says the meaning of faith is belief in God or in the Scriptures or other religious writings. Another meaning says belief without need of certain proof. Why is it that we have to be shown something before we will believe it?

What's funny is that some people see things and they still don't believe. To them it must have been a trick.

My husband, Thomas, didn't get to see our precious daughter until she was six months old because he was in Viet Nam. He found out he had a daughter in his mother's letter on St. Patrick's Day. I had written him but he got his moms letter first.

How many times have you gotten out those photo albums and looked at them? I am so thankful that I took the pictures that I have so I can look back on and remember the great times I shared with my loved ones or friends. I know some of the pictures can make us laugh or they can make us cry. But that is okay. That's what memories are for.

I can tell you that with God's help you can move forward instead of backward. You cannot do it on your own. I'm sure you have tried and it seemed like you almost made it but then the tears and pain crept back in.

You didn't want to go to bed because your loved one wasn't there to share it with you. For some reason the pain and loneliness seems to be worse at night. You can pretty well keep yourself busy during the day but it is when the night time comes that reality sets in.

Thomas and I went to the cemetery every day to see Cindy's grave. Our hearts were broken and we just wanted to be near her. But God told me one day, she is not there. Her shell is there but her soul is with me.

Cindy is in heaven with Jesus and she is not in pain and she is happy.

God is so good. I didn't need proof that Cindy was in heaven but God allowed Cindy to speak to me while I was dreaming. It happened a few days after her death. I was dreaming about something, nothing in particular, when I stopped dreaming and I saw Cindy's face and she said, "Mama, I'm alright, I'm happy. One day we will be together". Then I went back to the dream I was having.

I'm not telling you to not go to the cemetery and place flowers on your loved ones grave. I still go to Cindy's grave but I'm not making a shrine out of it. Flowers to me are a symbol of our love and represent to us how very much we miss our loved ones.

My best friend, Judy Tino, lost her precious husband, Ron, on March 11th, 2001. He had been sick for a long time. What I remember about Ron was that he served God with all his heart. He never judged. You could sit down and talk with him and he would really listen to you and after you said what you had to say, Ron would quietly tell you, not what you should do, but what the Bible said you should do. He knew his Bible. You could talk to him about politics or religion and he never got mad. He brought out the Bible and could tell you how God wants us to read the Bible and try and help other people who need love and support.

Judy and I try to get together on Friday nights for a few hours and catch up. She has my favorite chair and pillow there for me and yes we gossip some. We mostly talk about what has been happening in the world. But we also talk about God and the Bible. Judy is the type of friend that will be honest and open with you. Sadly, we were apart for four years but God brought us back together and I will not allow that to happen again.

People, when you can find a friend that will always be there for you through thick and thin, hold on to that friend and don't ever let go. If you do you will regret it. I love you, Judy.

God gave us his word to lead and guide us. He gave us his book which in itself is one big love letter. It also tells us how to live daily and love others. All we have to do is consult his book. We read everything else under the sun why not God's word?

Let me give you an example of finally trusting in God to help me with cigarettes.

I tried to justify smoking cigarettes. I ask God was it wrong to smoke cigarettes? Other than getting cancer what was the problem with smoking? I enjoyed the taste like most people did. I liked to have a cigarette after eating a meal. Then like a light going off in my head, which was God, I realized that if I had to ask then it was wrong.

I feel as Christians if we have to ask about whether we should do something or not then we should realize that it is wrong to begin with. Also, how could I be a witness for the Lord and stand there and puff on a cigarette and tell others about what Jesus had done for me? Think about it.

My sister, Barbara, died from COPD. She smoked for years. On one occasion when I was there at the hospital to see Barbara, she had been put on a respirator and the machine was pulling black gook out of her lungs. I had never seen anything like what I saw that day. It was like black tar. The nurse told me that the gook I was seeing was only coming from the top of Barbara's lungs. They couldn't get the tube to go down to the bottom because the gook was so thick. It was horrible.

While I was there I did ask my sister to squeeze my hand if she had ask God to forgive her of her sins and come into her heart and save her soul. A tear rolled down her cheek and she squeezed my hand. Praise God.

Well, maybe you need to sit down and write God a letter about how you have struggled to put the cigarettes down but you can't seem to do it. God can deliver me or you from whatever it is that bounds us. It might be too hard for you to say the words but just maybe putting them on paper would be easier. Why don't you try? What is keeping you from doing it? What can it hurt? It may even help.

There is nothing that my God cannot do. He can deliver you from cigarettes, drinking, drugs and anything else the devil throws at you. His power is awesome. If anyone ever tells you that you cannot get rid of something or someone that has you in bondage they are a liar! I know a man that can!

You are probably saying right about now, what does this have to do with the letter to God? I am going to get to the letter just hang on a little longer. I assure you it is coming. I don't want this book to be the shortest book in history.

I'm sure a lot of you will not like some of the things I have to say in my book. Well, if you have a problem with it then you will have to take it up with God or you could pick the book up, skim threw it and if you don't like what you've read, put it down and pretend you didn't read it. Makes sense to me.

And don't try and tell me you have never done that before. Oh, yes, you have. I have especially at the grocery store. When we are in a line at the grocery store we tend to grab a magazine, browse through it and then put it back when we are ready to check out. That way we don't feel guilty about not buying it. I admit I have done it. It's just human nature to do it.

Hey, I like to read a good book too. I usually read the back cover to see what the book is about. If it sounds pretty good I usually buy it. If I don't think I am going to like it I read the ending and put it back. Sound familiar?

Speaking of New York, my husband, Thomas, and I had never been to the Big Apple. We had always wanted to go but after we checked into the air fare and the hotels, we decided it was just too expensive. But God opened the door for us to go. If you ever get the opportunity to go to New York you really should go.

Now, if you don't like crowds and a lot of walking you may not like it. I have never seen so many people on one street and going the same way in my life. We didn't let a little thing like rain bother us or even a down pour. People, that's what raincoats and umbrellas are for. I also have 642 pictures to prove it.

Since we are on the subject of rain I have to tell you this. It is cute. You or your parents may have said the same thing to someone else at some point in your life.

My uncle Roy came to our house and wanted my mother to go to Rutherford with him and his wife, Polly, and see their brother and his family. Well, naturally it was raining that day. My mom said that she couldn't go because it was raining outside. *My uncle Roy said, it ain't raining in my car"*. And yes the word "ain't" is in Webster. I figure if it is in Webster then it has to be a word right?

My computer highlighted it and said it wasn't spelled correctly. My computer needs to check with Webster. If you don't believe me look it up.

Okay, back to New York. I would like to give you a little advice if you are ever on the streets of New York and you decide to stop walking. Don't do it. That could be dangerous to your health.

I found the people in New York walking on the streets, do not stop, even while they are texting and talking on the phone or both unless they are at the corner and that is only because they are waiting for the sign to tell them that they can walk.

But it is truly amazing to see the people just go around you if you make a sudden stop. It's like it is a natural thing for them to do that is if you are a New Yorker. If you don't live in New York I recommend you know exactly where you are going or don't go.

Following the person ahead of you could get you lost so I wouldn't suggest doing that. They may not know where they are going either. And you better know your street signs and north from south and east from west, which I do not. If you look around you should see a policeman. I'm sure they are used to people asking them directions. Praying helps too.

I would not drive in New York for any amount of money. Our driver, Tony, made a left turn and I looked down and it was unreal as to how close he came to that pole. I could never have done it. But I guess he had driven a lot in New York and other cities that he knew how much space he had. I admit I held my breath. Thank you Tony for taking such good care of us.

I don't know about your husband but mine does not like to ask for directions. He had rather get lost than to ask for directions. I must tell you this just for some food for thought.

This happened several years ago. Naturally, we were lost and I told my husband to stop at the little store we saw up on the right of the road and ask for directions.

I told him the person working there should be able to help us because they probably lived around here. Get ready-----here it comes. He said "he don't know any more than I do. I can tell by looking at him". I really, really hate to admit this but the man wasn't from around there and he didn't know either. Now we have a GPS. If you don't have one you better get one. They are really neat. Now if I just could figure out how to use it!

Okay, back to New York again. We left on my birthday, December 5th, and we returned on Thursday night. Thomas and I had a great time and the other people on the bus were fantastic. We laughed and ate all the way going and coming. I have never laughed so much in my life. I am not going to admit how much I ate either. The goodies were too awesome to pass up. It was good clean Christian fun.

For some reason some people think you have to do something dirty to have fun. That just isn't so. We watched Christian movies and sang Christmas songs. When God is in it everything turns out wonderful.

I have never figured it out when some people say they have to get drunk to have a good time. Can't you be yourself without having to drink and get drunk? Or is that why you drink to be someone you truly are not. Does drinking give you courage to say things you normally wouldn't say or do? How does waking up with a headache in the morning and not remembering what you did the night before help you?

Oh, now you are saying I am judging. Well, like I said before take it up with God. He said it in his word. Sometimes the truth hurts. Or is that why you don't want to read the word of God?

While I am on the subject there is something else I can't seem to understand. People tell their children that they cannot smoke or drink yet they do it in front of them. I heard one of my own relatives tell their children they had to wait until they were older. Right, wait till you are older to get lung cancer or liver cancer. Are they saying you don't want to get cancer while you are young? You should wait until you are older so then you will have better sense? Will they? God's word says in Proverbs 22:6 (KJV) *"train up a child in the way he should go; and when he is old, he will not depart from it"*.

What kind of examples are we showing our children? I believe if we strive to live a good Christian life in front of our children and grandchildren they will want to live a good life too.

People, children remember things from when they were small. They pick up every little word you say. Don't you remember doing the same thing when you were small?

When we were growing up we did not curse in our home. Our parents said they would wash out our mouths with soap. My mama got all up set it we said dern. Maybe we need this in our homes even today.

Guess what? I couldn't find the word dern in Webster. Then I wonder why my mama got so upset? An adult thing I guess.

What has happened to the word respect? How as adults can we expect to get respect from our children when we won't even give that same respect to them?

If you want to see a child's face light up tell them how great they did in picking up their toys or how good they did in school.

Have you ever stood at your four or five year old child's bed and listened to them pray? Sometimes you have to put your hand over your mouth to keep from crying. They are so sincere when they pray. They even pray for the cat or dog. There is not one mean bone in their body.

Why do adults smack their children across the room for cursing when they themselves curse in front of their children? Oh, maybe it is an adult thing. People, something is terribly wrong in our homes today.

If a person hurts a child of God and I'm not just talking about a Christian, God will get you. You can count on it. It may not be today or tomorrow or a year from now, but the Bible says "vengeance is mine, I will repay." (Romans12:1KJV).

A very dear pastor, Rev. Leo Kuykendall, whom I love with all my heart, once said, "That God doesn't always pay off on Friday". God is a just God and a loving

God but he will not allow his precious little ones to be hurt.

I'm not a preacher and I don't claim to be one. But I have read my Bible and it doesn't lie. God cannot lie either. Haven't you heard what goes around comes around?

Okay, before I forget, let me tell you a few interesting facts I did not know about New York. First, let me tell you that going to New York and seeing it up close and personal really changed my mind of how I thought New York would be.

In the movies you see the cities run by mobsters and the homeless everywhere on the streets. I did not see any homeless people. Now for the mob, well, that could be a different story. I didn't stop to look for any guys with hats and trench coats for fear of getting run over.

I did not know that you could be given a ticket for blowing your horn. I kid you not. The police would be working overtime here in my town just giving out tickets for that. There are signs on the street corners that say Don't Honk.

There was also one sign that read Do Not Block the Box. This box was what would make the lights turn for the traffic. If you blocked this box you would get a fine, I believe the fine was $350.00, and you would also get two points taken off your license. I tell you these people don't fool around. They mean business.

Something else to keep in mind is that if you have a "fender bender" you better not call the police because they will not come out. You have to file the claim with your own insurance company. Isn't it great to learn things that you didn't know?

We got to see the Radio City Christmas Spectacular starring The Rockettes perform and they were so good. They never missed a step. In one section of the show where they were dressed up like soldiers all the Rockettes lined up and then the one at the first of the line starts to fall and then the next one and so on. It was truly amazing. But the part I loved the most was the last of the show where the story of Christmas was displayed. Mary, Joseph and the baby Jesus were shown along with the three wise men and two camels and a little donkey.

I kept thanking Jesus for these people and this show. A lot of shows will not allow anything pertaining to Jesus for fear of upsetting some people. It did not upset me in the least! In fact I loved it. God bless that show and the people who performed in it.

If someone got offended all they had to do was get up and leave. I would really have hated to see somebody get upset and have to leave because of such a wonderful show. They would've missed a blessing.

Have you noticed how in this day and age people get offended so easily?

The most overwhelming place we saw was ground zero. We were the first group to be allowed to go into the area and see ground zero. In the days previous to our group people had to go into buildings nearby and look down to see it. They were not allowed to go right up to the area. Security was also very tight.

If you can go there and you are not touched in some way please, go back again. To some it may just have been a place to take pictures and take up their time and be able to say they actually got to see where it all happened. I believe once you actually see it, your life will be changed forever.

Ground Zero is a part of our history. It's not a bedtime story for little children. When I saw it on television that day I was shocked. I'm sure you were too. You don't see something this horrible on television every day.

What I didn't understand is why did the news media keep showing it over and over again even days and weeks after it happened? Didn't they know that the families had those horrific scenes embedded in their minds without the news media showing it to them every time the television channels came on? Yes, they could've changed the channel but it was being played on just about every channel. What if that had been your precious loved one?

Ground Zero is not just a place to take pictures and say you were there. I assure you it wasn't to the families who lost their loved ones. You cannot help but be touched by your surroundings.

When I started to walk up to the area where the Twin Towers used to be I could feel my heart beat faster and I wanted to just stand there and take it all in. I could feel a calmness in the air. I felt God there.

I did not know anyone that had lost their lives that day and yet I felt like I had known them all. I felt the pain that their loved ones had felt and are still feeling. I said a silent prayer for the loved ones that God would give them peace in their hearts and comfort them as only he can.

I know the pain and heartache they feel will continue to be with them until they leave this earth. There was no reason for the men, women and children to lose their lives that day.

Have you ever looked up the word "hate"? I went to Webster and looked it up. It means to regard with extreme aversion, detest. The dictionary also said it means to feel hatred. I cannot image a person having so much hatred toward another person to want to kill that person and everyone else close to them. Hate is a very strong word. It only has four letters. How can four letters be so powerful? It's how you say or write them that makes them powerful.

Don't try and tell me you have never said the word hate to someone. I know you have because I have. When I was little I would tell my sisters that I hated them because they would never let me go with them or play with them. It may have had something to do with the fact that I would tell on them which I usually did.

Haven't you told your parents you hated them for not getting to go out with the boy of your dreams? Aren't you glad they were right and you were wrong about him? Yes, people I was young once. Believe it or not parents do know best. We've been there and done that too. And yes we do understand.

If you had written your parents a letter telling them how you felt about not being allowed to do what you wanted to what would you have said? Would your words have hurt them?

Don't wait till your loved ones or that friend passes away. Write them a letter now. Maybe it has been years but it is never too late. The Bible says love is patient and love is kind.

Even if your loved ones have passed away why don't you sit down and write them a letter? What can it hurt? Tell them all the things you wanted to say to them when they were living. Put the letter in your safe and give it to your children when they get older.

Doctors tell us when we talk things out it makes us feel better. Well, I believe putting words on paper can be a good way to do that. I did it.

Another thing you could do is get two chairs and you sit down in one of them and put the other chair in front of you. Now, you pretend the person you want to talk to is in that other chair. What would you say? Let your words come from your heart and not your head. Say all those things you wanted to say but you didn't. Be honest, don't lie. It's just you and that chair there.

You might want to have a notepad and pen or pencil in your hand just in case you would want to remember some of the things you said to that person. You could write your letter and keep it for later on when you feel lonely and nobody is there but you and your letter. Words are memories too. They are just written on paper.

Remember that word hate? Would you be willing to give your life for someone whom you knew hated you? You knew for a fact that you were hated by people all over the world. I know a man who would and did give his life for every person that has ever lived, is living and will live in the future. I'll tell you more about this wonderful man later on before we get to the letter.

If you saw the movie where the guy, Greg Kenner, worked at the post office and then letters started to come in for the Easter Bunny, Santa Claus and God then you know how many different letters the post office gets each day. I believe he helped answer them. If I am not mistaken he especially answered the ones to God. The letters that came in to the post office went to the "dead letters" bins.

If the post office didn't know where to send these letters they would put them in these bins. He got into a lot of trouble but it all turned out for the best in the end. Sorry, if I gave away the ending. You could still get the movie and watch it.

The Lord put this thought in my mind and I just had to write it down. I'm sure you have thought about writing a letter and maybe the letter you thought about writing was to a loved one, a friend or someone you met recently and you wanted to drop them a line or two and find out how they were doing. You probably wanted to let them know how you and your family were doing.

I've noticed that when I sit down to write a letter it is not as easy as I would have thought it would be. Why is it so hard to write a letter?

Now, if it is a thank you note you pretty well know what you are going to write. If you received a birthday present naturally you would want to thank the person that sent it to you. It's really not hard to say thank you.

But if you got say, a tie, especially one that you already had, it would be a short note. I'm using an example for a man because I'm not about to hurt a woman's feelings. I'm only kidding. I will probably get hate mail from men. Sorry guys.

But it is entirely different when it comes to a letter. You could make it really short and say, "Hi, miss you, write soon". I do that on my email. Have you found yourself doing that too?

Letters are us, our inner self except on paper. Sometimes we can write a letter better than we can talk to a person. Wonder why that is? We should try and put our words in a loving way. Please, don't be mean when you write a letter. If you plan to then just don't write it.

If you are writing a business letter you may not have too much trouble in finding the write, no pun intended, words to express to the person you are writing to. You simply write what needs to be written and you are through with the letter.

I know it is easier to pick up the phone and call the person, but how many of us think about it for a minute or two and then change our minds and say we will call them later?

Our excuse is we need to do something else and we just don't have the time. But we seem to find the time to do something else. Don't we?

Our words can hurt and once they come out of our mouths we cannot take those words back. We can try and explain that we really didn't mean what we said but the other person knows what they heard.

Once you write the words on paper the letter can be torn up, thrown away and destroyed but you still remember those words you put down on that paper. They will forever be imprinted in your mind and heart.

Does this sound familiar but why must I always be the first one to pick up the phone or write the letter? They have fingers too. Let them do it for once. It always has to be me taking the first step. It just isn't fair to me. Let them buy the paper, envelope and stamp this time. I have too so let them do it too.

Be honest, don't we all feel this way at some point in our lives? The truth hurts but the truth will always stand.

What about when they do make the call and you really don't want to hear what they have to say. Don't they know I have feelings too?

How many times have we let the answering machine get the calls? We don't want to talk right now, our favorite show is on. I have problems of my own. I don't want to listen to theirs. I'll call them back later.

People, I know what I am talking about because I have done the same thing. I have to pray a lot and ask God to forgive me. I'm human too.

You might say, when I write a letter I don't have to talk to the person face to face. If I need to say something that I cannot tell them to their face, I can put it down on paper. That way I don't hurt anyone.

And besides I may not see that person for years so I don't have to worry about what I write down. And if I do see them I can just say I don't really remember that letter. Makes sense to me.

But what if they kept the letter and decided not to throw it in the trash? Now that could be a problem. I guess I could always apologize and then they would have to forgive me. The good book says they have too. So that makes it okay doesn't it?

Did you know that God wrote a letter also? He wrote a love letter. Yes, he did. You can find it in John 3:16(KJV). It was the most beautiful letter ever written. He let man put it to paper so it would always be there for us to read and always remember what Jesus did for us. That was 2,000 years ago.

It doesn't take a well known writer to write a letter. Most people can write a letter but it is what they put in that letter that will make a difference in other peoples' lives.

God's letter is from his heart and with sincere love. It goes like this, "For God so loved the world that he gave his only begotten son, that whosoever believeth in him should not perish but have everlasting life". This is not only a letter but a promise. We tend to break our promises, sometimes not really meaning too, but God never breaks his promises. He cannot lie. Oh, how I wish I could say that.

David also wrote God a letter and it is in the Twenty-Third Psalm. It is beautiful and from his heart.

No one on this earth is perfect only Jesus Christ. When he tells us he is going to do something, he means it. If he has told you to write a letter to a loved one or friend that you have hurt in some way, you better do it. God will not let you rest until you do. Been there done that. I know what I am talking about.

Are you lonely? Why don't you sit down and write God a letter and tell him how lonely you are? Tell him about how you would love to see more of your family, your children and your grandchildren. Tell God how you would love to get a card or just a short letter from them.

Tell God how you sit and wait for the phone to ring so you can hear their voice. You just want to know they care.

Did you hurt them in some way or did they hurt you somehow? God will listen when nobody else will. God will read your letter and he will answer because he sees those tears as they fall down your cheek. Let it go. Whatever it is it's not worth losing your loved ones or friends. Please, don't let pride stand in your way. Write them first or call them first. Believe me you will feel so much better.

Did you know that there is a machine out there and it is called a tape recorder. You can talk on it. If you cannot write a letter for whatever reason get you a tape recorder and make a tape and send it to the family member or the friend. There are too many different items on the market that you could use, so quit making excuses.

I heard a preacher say that the story goes that a woman went up to her pastor and was just a crying and asked her pastor to pray for this lady that she was dying with cancer. The pastor found out later that the lady who had cancer was a character on a soap opera.

My mama use to get so mad at her sister over those soap operas. Mama always seemed to call her when

General Hospital was on. So mama either called her before it came on or after it went off that way she knew she could talk to her. Mama made fun of her watching those soaps.

We never seem to run out of things to talk about when we get on the phone. Sometimes we talk so long that we have to hang up because our voice starts to crack and our ear starts to go numb. It's just a plain fact.

Don't be surprised if I tend to go back and forth. It's called old age. Don't worry you will have problems when you get older. You won't get left out.

Is it not strange that when we write a letter to someone we have to really think of what to say? Once we start writing the letter we find that we have run out of things to say. We can just say so much about our family.

When my husband, Thomas, was in Vietnam I found all kinds of things to write about at first. He was going to be over there in that foreign country for one whole year.

In the beginning I had all kinds of things to say. You know how it is with young people. I told him how much I missed him and loved him.

I was pregnant when he left so I talked about our baby. We did not know if we were having a girl or boy. You didn't have the advantage of having a sonogram done to know so you could have a shower knowing what the babies' gender was going to be. Some of you know what I am talking about. I know I am old but you are too. So it was not too hard to come up with things to write to Thomas about and not keep repeating myself.

My letters were long at first and after a while they got a little shorter because I was starting to run out of things to say. There is just so much you can say about the weather and not make it boring.

Thomas wrote long letters too. He had a lot to say about what all he was doing. He could not say where he was because the Army read the letters going out and the letters that were coming in to him. I bet they got tired or reading about how much I loved him and missed him. They probably got bored ready all the letters that came in and went out not just mine but the other letters that the wives, moms and relatives wrote to their loved ones in Vietnam.

I know he got tired of hearing the same old thing over and over. But I just had so much I could write about. It would've been nice to have had a fancy typewriter to type with. But unfortunately they had not been invented then. Today I can type on the computer and go pretty fast. The computer is mightier than the pen.

I did write to him about the different groups that were out at that time. I especially loved the Beatles. This was music that you could understand what they were saying. The words talked about love, people and the world. Today's music is a lot of screaming and cursing. It is so loud. I cannot understand half of what they are singing about. But didn't they have to write the lyrics down on paper?

The younger generation probably thinks I am crazy and not on the same planet but one thing I know for a fact is my husband loved to listen to that music. When I was dating him he had a stereo system not a boom box in his bedroom and he would love to listen to music after he got off work.

Having bombs blow up all around him while he was in Vietnam and the spraying of Agent Orange caused him to go completely deaf. He has to wear two hearing aids now and still says to me "what did you say"?

My husband told me that when he first arrived in Vietnam, they had to build a runway for the planes and that when the Army got in different items for the men or equipment that those items came in cardboard boxes. Once the boxes where opened the men would throw out the card board boxes and leave them in a pile along the road. The Vietnamese people would fight over the cardboard boxes because they would use them as a house to protect themselves from the rain. Can you image having to do that? We are so blessed by God.

He also said there weren't any dogs over there either. The people ate them. We need to get down on our knees and thank God for what we have. We are so blessed and do not even realize it. We need to praise God everyday for what we have.

Opening my eyes and getting up of a morning is to me a blessing in itself. Wait until those bones of yours go to aching and you hurt all over. Having good health is really a blessing. Just wait until you have to start taking all those pills of a morning. They are not all the same color either and some of them are very big. Friend, there is a pill box in a drug store somewhere out there with your name on it.

Because of having to take so many pills, I have had to have my throat stretched three times. After the third time the doctor told me I needed to have my throat re-built. That's not fun at all. God was there and brought me through it. I praise him for it.

Young people of today will say they are so tired of hearing us old folks talk about the way we use to live. What in the world would they do without radio, television or loud music? What if the power went out for long periods of time? Think of not having any batteries! Oh my word.

Have they ever had to cook on a wooden stove? Why is that you ask? Don't we old people know about microwaves? Yes, and we would've used them if they had been invented.

And what if they had to sleep in a bedroom with no heat and only seven or eight blankets to cover them up with?

Girls, what if you only had one or two dresses to wear and they weren't Vera Wang? And no makeup!

Don't forget those big screen televisions. I remember watching shows on a twenty inch screen. Talk about small that was small. But now we have those big screen televisions that take up about half of your living room. But you can see the pictures. No doubt about that. Yes, I am old, 62 to be exact, but just remember the older I get the older you get.

What would the younger generation do without those IPods and the phones that do everything for them? Now they can take pictures instantly and send them to their friends and put them on the internet for the whole world and their brothers to see. Isn't that wonderful to know?

I think it is scary to be able to do that. We are opening up our lives to anybody. You know as well as I do that people can get into your email and face book and find out things about you that you may not want them to know. Isn't modern technology wonderful?

But what if all this were taken away and never to be seen again? Would it really be all that bad?

My husband told me that the guys in Viet Nam couldn't wait until mail call. They were so eager to hear from their wives and families. To them their mail was more precious than gold.

But there was one letter they didn't want to ever get. This was the "Dear John" letter. My heart goes out to the men and women while in service and away from home that got a "Dear John" letter. That would have to be the saddest letter they had ever gotten. No one should ever have to get that type of letter no matter where they happen to be. Only God could give the comfort and love that they would need to get through such a tragic ordeal as that.

My husband told me about some of the guys in his platoon that got that type of letter. He said one guy took out his gun and shot and killed himself. I couldn't image why the woman couldn't wait till her husband or boyfriend got home to tell him.

Please, pray for our service people. They are fighting for our freedom even today in foreign countries. They are under more stress than we could ever image. They need all our love and support that we can give them. I thank God that I have never had to see or go through what they are facing today. God hears and answers prayers. If you don't believe me just try it. God might just surprise you.

Friends, I wrote about the trees, the weather, and my back pain. I told him all my pain was his fault. I would talk about his mom and dad, not literally, just about how they were so I would have something to talk about. There is just so much you can put in a letter and not repeat yourself which I did. There comes a point and time that I just ran out of things to talk about. I was not working so I couldn't talk about my job. I told him about my mom and dad and about my sisters and their families.

When my family gave me a baby shower I talked about it and all the boys and girls clothes I got. I took some pictures and sent them to him. I think at the time I had a Polaroid camera. Remember those cameras?

Now, that was the thing to have and take pictures with. Instant pictures! I also think I had a black and white camera too. If I remember right it was a Kodak 110 camera. You have to remember that was back in 1969. "You've come a long way baby".

Some of us may wish these cameras were back since the companies have put so many new gadgets on the cameras we now have. At least with the instant cameras you snapped the picture and out it came. Then you got to see the picture in a few minutes even if it was blurred. Some of you may still have one or both of these cameras lying around somewhere.

Sometimes you get distracted and forget what you were saying or in this case writing. Please, don't try and say you don't. I'm sure you have in the past when you wrote someone a letter. I tried to proof read my letters before I sent them.

What is wrong with writing a letter to God? God answers our letters in the form of prayers. God has never failed to answer my prayers. I just have to wait on him. The Bible says to "be patient and wait on the Lord". I really need to work on that part.

We write letters to others about different things. Don't you like it when the person answers your letter? We all love to get letters. I know I do. I'm just not very good at writing them. I confess.

We send wedding invitations, baby shower invitations, anniversary invitations and graduation cards. We don't seem to have a problem in sending these out in the mail.

Let's be honest for a minute. Haven't you gotten something in the mail and looked at it and threw it away because it didn't interest you at the time? Some of the mail I get I don't even open it I just throw it in the trash can. Especially those Publisher's Clearing House. I know I will never win that. I really wonder sometimes if it has to do with the fact that I never order any of those magazines in the brochure. Have you ever noticed how they will send you another one and tell you this is your last chance but you still keep getting them?

Don't we let our children write letters to Santa Clause? They will tell him what they want for Christmas. They are so sweet. Their little hearts are so tender.

Don't you just love it when the children will ask how does Santa get down their chimney?

I can remember asking our parents how did Santa bring our toys to us because we did not have a chimney for him to climb down. My sisters and I were told that he had a key to our door. We believed that. It made sense to us.

Why can't they write to Jesus and tell him about their mommies and daddies and ask him to help their parents to find a job? Little children are so sincere when they pray.

We let them say their prayers at night so why can't they write to Jesus? They write to Santa once a year but they can write to Jesus or pray every day if they want too.

Isn't it wonderful that Jesus comes more than once a year? He is here all the time.

Jesus says in Matthew 19:14(KJV) "suffer little children and forbid them not to come unto me: for such is the kingdom of heaven". God loves to hear his precious little boys and girls pray. Their hearts are so tender. They are so innocent and are so sincere when they pray. We should strive to try encourage our children to pray for their family and friends.

Children love to write cards and letters to grandma and grandpa. They especially love to get cards from them too. My grandson, Christopher, loves to get mail. He wants to go to the mailbox with his dad, Scott, and help him get the mail. I try and send him cards that I make myself. He loves those. When is the last time you sent your grandchild a card?

How many times have you started a letter and then tore it up and threw it in the trash? Did you ever stop and think that maybe that person or loved one needed to get that letter? You never know it could be a blessing to them to get it. But what if it hurts them instead of helps them? Maybe we need to pray and ask God to help us in writing the letter before we send it to them.

We should never try to intentionally hurt the ones we love. Our lips are like a two edged sword and our words.

can be too whether we say them or write them down on paper.

Once we say something that will hurt someone we cannot take those words back neither can we take back the words we put on paper. Remember the letters or cards you write should come from your heart. Let God lead you before you mail it because he always loves.

God wants us to help people and not hurt them. We truly only hurt ourselves when we set out to hurt others. We should love and not condemn. That's not our job. God will take care of that for us. I want to be a blessing and make people feel good. *My mama use to say, "what goes around comes around".* I truly believe that.

Remember those school days when you were in love with a classmate? I remember it being called "puppy love".

Do you remember that note you gave a friend of yours to give to the boy you liked in elementary school? Come on, remember that? Remember how you saw him read the note and then throw it into the trash can? It broke your heart because he didn't even acknowledge to you that he got it. But the good thing is you probably didn't marry him and you are glad.

My husband writes me a love note on a 4X5 piece of paper every morning before he goes to work. He puts the note down inside my pocket book. I take it out and read it and then put the notes in a shoe box and put the box under our bed. I have about four boxes of them.

He has been writing the notes to me for about ten years. I kid you not. I look forward to those notes. I wouldn't take a million dollars for them.

Ladies, why don't you start writing your hubby a note and putting the note where you know he will find it? If he wears a hat put the note in it. Give him the shock of his life. You never know you might just start getting one too. What can it hurt?

I have tried to imagine what a letter from a child would be like that would write a letter to God. I think it would go something like this. Dear God: what do you look like? Do you have a white beard? Do you wear glasses? What kind of games do you play? How old are you? Why do I have to eat all my vegetables? Can you fly? Why does my brother cry all the time? Why does Nana kiss me on the face all the time?

I think the world would be a better place if we could all be as humble as a child. Haven't you ever noticed how children can get mad at each other but be friends again in just a few minutes? They can forgive and forget real easy. Can we as adults do the same? We should.

God wants us to be kind to each other. When we see a homeless person on the street do we try and avoid them or just give them a few dollars so they will go away? We truly don't know the reason they are there. There are probably a lot of people that do not want to be out on the street. Things may have happened in their lives that caused this to happen to them. We should not judge them. Friends, we never know that could be us out there.

God loves them just as much as he loves us. Maybe they are on the street so we can show them kindness and love. Wouldn't you want someone to be nice to you if it were you in their shoes?

If that person uses the money you gave them for the wrong reasons, they will have to answer to God not you. You gave from your heart that's all that matters.

I thank God every day for all his blessings to me and my family. He has been so good to me. I fail him every day but all I have to do is pray and ask for forgiveness and repent and he forgives me.

I can remember a time when my dad went to the grocery store and charged a pound of liver mush so we could make us a sandwich. I'm not trying to give you a sob story. I'm telling you how God supplied our need even if it was liver mush.

There is a man that loves you unconditionally. He will always be there for you no matter what comes your way. He loves to hear from you and me when we pray. His line is never busy. He won't scream and holler at you. He is always loving and kind. He shows mercy instead of hate. He knows your pain.

He loved us so much that he sent his only begotten Son to come to earth and die for our sins so we could go to be with him for all eternity. His name is Jesus. He was born to die. What is so beautiful about this is that he freely gave his life for us. He wasn't made to do it John 3:16(KJV).

Oh, yes, I must tell you this too. This has probably happened to you. We lived on Washington Street when we were little. The reason I remember this so well is because we had a dog and daddy took it off one day when we weren't there and he set the dog out. When we found out we cried our little hearts out.

About two weeks later we were sitting at the table eating dinner and we heard a barking and scratching at the back door. There was our dog soaking wet and wagging his tail. I wish I could remember his name. But my dad said he would never do that again.

God knew we missed that dog and he brought that dog back home to us. God hears and answers prayer. He is the same yesterday, today and forever.

I also want to mention that I read Rev. Billy Graham's new book <u>Nearing Home</u>. If you haven't read his book please do. This is really a great book. It will bless your soul. It has really helped me in seeing what lays ahead for God's children.

People, the saved and born again will walk on streets of gold. We won't ever grow old or be sick ever again. We will never cry another tear. We won't ever have to go to the cemetery either. We will get to see and be with our loved ones who have gone on before us.

We don't know why bad things happen but when we get to Heaven I don't think we will care. We will be too happy.

God has given us a free will. He will never make us do something we don't want to do. But he could help us to change our minds if he sees the path we are on could harm us. If he does it will be for his glory and not ours.

Well, it's time to mention the letter I told you about at the beginning of the book.

Why write a letter to God? We know we can't mail it to him. Why even take the time?

Do you have some item that maybe was given to you and is very precious to you and you have it hidden in a special place? That's why I think writing a letter to God and keeping it in a safe place to re-read as often as you want too would be precious to you.

On those rainy cold days when you are by yourself, you could get out your letter to God and read it. You could get comfort from that letter. It could even put a smile on your face.

God wants to hear from you and me whether it is in a prayer or in a letter. To me a letter would be your silent prayer on paper to keep and read.

Tell God how you feel. If you can't say it in words than write it down in your own words on paper. What would be wrong in doing that? It would be just between you and God. Nobody has to see it or read it unless you want them too.

I wish I had taken my own advice many years ago when a relative was on drugs and set down and wrote a letter to God. I wish I had poured my heart out and ask God to help me to help her. Her habit not only hurt her it almost destroyed all the people who loved her. She just couldn't understand that we were trying to help her.

Friends, if you have a loved one on drugs you cannot help them until they ask for that help. I did so many things wrong. I needed to turn her over to God and not judge her.

I truly believe if I had written God that letter then I could've seen my own mistakes. Seeing the words on paper could've made a big difference.

Don't wait like I did. I waited too late. She died as a result of using a dirty needle for her drugs.

My letter to God has been in this book I am writing to you. My letter is personal to me just like your letter would be to you. Your letter to God would also be as unique to you as mine is to me.

This whole book is my letter to God and to you. It is written from my heart. I want my letter to be a blessing to you. Friend, you are not alone.

Like I said God wants to hear from us. Let him hear from you. Write from your heart. Pour out your heart to God. Tell him what you are going through. Tell him about your pain.

Put your letter in your special hiding place. Maybe for you it would be your Bible. This way it would be easier for you to remember where you put your letter.

You know you could write two letters. One to that person you love and haven't heard from in a while and one to God.

I'm sure that there is someone in your life that you have wanted to write a letter to but you just haven't taken the time to do it. I encourage you to take that step and write that person. You might get a reply in the mail. Don't email them. Write them a letter. You may not want the whole world to read it.

Friends, time is short. When you do decide to write that letter, it may be too late. Remember, we are not promised tomorrow.

Today is the time.

I pray that God will bless you and your family each and every day.

My prayer is that you will come to know Christ as your personal Saviour before you finish this book.

Linda lives in Gastonia, North Carolina with her husband, Thomas and her Boston Terrier Georgia. She has been married for 43 years.

She has another book, It's Okay to Hurt-My Life with Fibromyalgia. She has had this invisible painful disease for 28 years. God encouraged her to write this book to help others.

She has written this book to help and inspire people to have a closer walk with God.

Did you know that you don't have to have paper to write a letter? God doesn't care if it is written on notebook paper or cardboard paper. God wants to hear from you.

One day when you are feeling so lonely and broken hearted write God a letter. He truly wants to hear from you. He can comfort you when nobody else can.

Do you think it would be silly to write God a letter? Why?

I assure you that God will answer that letter through prayer. That's his way of answering you back.